THE CAREER LAB FORMULA

8 Easy Steps to Get You From College to a Career In STEM

SIDDHI SHAH

The Career Lab Formula: 8 Easy Steps to Get You From College to a Career In STEM by Siddhi Shah is published by Siddhi Shah LLC.

© 2021 Siddhi Shah LLC, First Edition

All rights reserved. This book or parts thereof may not be reproduced in any form, stored in any retrieval system or transmitted in any form by any means – electronic, mechanical, photocopy, recording, or otherwise – without prior written permission of the publisher, except as provided by United States of America copyright law.

Disclaimer:

This content provided herein are simply for educational purposes. Every effort has been made to ensure that the information provided in this book is accurate and helpful for our readers at time of publishing. However, this is not an exhaustive treatment of the subject. The author and publisher do not assume and hereby claim any liability to any party for any loss, damage or disruption caused by any errors or omissions whether such errors or omissions result from negligence, accident, or any other cause. You are responsible for your own choices, actions, and results.

Contents

Introduction v

STEP 1:
The Biggest Job Searching Secrets That No One Tells You .. 1

STEP 2:
The Basics: Creating a Resume
and a Cover Letter... 7

STEP 3:
Creating a LinkedIn Profile
(and Thoughts About Other Social Media Platforms)...... 23

STEP 4:
The Job Search Itself 29

STEP 5:
Networking and Asking For an Informational Interview ... 45

STEP 6:
Prepping For Interviews
(Phone, In-Person, and Virtual)............................ 53

STEP 7:
Compensation and Negotiating the Offer 71

STEP 8:
References, Background, and Drug Checks 79

Final Word 83

APPENDIX:
Sample Areas of Employment By Degree Type............ 85

About the Author..........................93

Introduction

According to the Education Commission of States, between 2017 and 2027, the number of Science, Technology, Engineering, or Math (STEM) jobs will grow 13% (versus 9% for non-STEM jobs).

And positions in computing, engineering, and advanced manufacturing are leading the way.

Fortunately for STEM graduates like you, earnings in these fields are high, and unemployment is low — because talent is limited *(so you're in demand!)*.

Despite this demand, many graduates have no idea what career to pursue and are unsure how to land a STEM job.

But have no fear…

The Career Lab Formula is here to help you do just that — land your first STEM job.

As a STEM graduate myself *(Bachelor's in Biology, MIT; Master's in Biotechnology, UPENN)* — I fully appreciate the unique dynamics and requirements associated with a STEM job search.

Furthermore, throughout my career as a Corporate Strategist with over 15 years of experience hiring recent graduates — and also volunteering as a career mentor at careercontessa.com and a former Board Member at Project Learn (an educational non-profit) — I understand how difficult it can be for graduates like you to land STEM jobs.

During my career, I've coached my successful Career Lab Formula to many graduate jobseekers who've found and secured their first STEM jobs.

But in 2020 — during the lockdowns in response to the COVID-19 pandemic — I decided I needed to expand my reach.

I asked myself, *How can I use my additional free time to help even more graduates get their first jobs?*

Then it hit me — I had to write a book.

And that's how *The Career Lab Formula: 8 Easy Steps to Get You From College to a Career In STEM* came to be — **through a desire to help graduates like you land your first career job without the need for direct consultation.**

The first full-time job a graduate takes after college tends to have a profound influence on the rest of their career.

Many graduates finish their bachelor's or master's in a STEM field, get so frustrated with the job application

Introduction

process, and end up working full-time in a job that has little to do with their area of study (or doesn't require a degree at all) for years.

Now, judging by the fact that you're reading this book, I'm guessing you're looking for a STEM-related career — not just any old job.

And that's great — because you're in the right place. *The Career Lab Formula: 8 Easy Steps to Get You From College to a Career In STEM* is a comprehensive, yet simplified process to help you land that first career job.

You may be asking, *But is The Career Lab Formula right for me?* And that's a great question.

So let's see if any of the following sounds familiar:

- You just finished college with a bachelor's or master's degree in STEM.

- During your senior year, you were so busy finishing your coursework, you didn't have much time to think about or work on job applications.

- Since you graduated, everyone has been bugging you nonstop with the question, have you got a job yet?

- With the career service office out of reach, you feel so overwhelmed about the job application process, and you've got no idea where to start.

- You've read (or thought about reading) various books, blogs, and websites. So far, they haven't provided the answers you need to land a STEM job.

If you find yourself nodding along to even one of these, then you're in luck — you're the exact type of person *The Career Lab Formula* is for.

But let's slow down a bit.

First, let's celebrate your wonderful achievement — congrats on finishing college! That's a major accomplishment. I hope you're super proud of yourself.

Let's keep this time joyous and not allow it to devolve into something stressful.

So take a deep breath... I — and *The Career Lab Formula* — have your back.

I said a similar thing to both my nephews, Razaad and Ross, when they finished their bachelor's degrees. And they used this formula to help them job hunt.

And guess what?

They both have STEM jobs they love.

Ross, a Chemical Engineering major, landed a role as a Manufacturing Associate at a Gene Therapy Contract Manufacturer after four months of job hunting. Two

Introduction

years after graduating, he's already on his second job out of college — now working for as a Process Engineer at a biotech start-up.

Razaad, a Chemistry graduate, spent about a year finding his dream STEM job as a Manufacturing Associate at a Diagnostic Company that played an integral role in delivering tests during the COVID-19 pandemic.

And now you've got the opportunity to achieve what my nephews and countless others have by reading and implementing the steps in this book.

First, I recommend you read *The Career Lab Formula: 8 Easy Steps to Get You From College to a Career In STEM* all the way through before you do the exercises.

Doing so will ensure you gain a fuller understanding of the process and appreciate how each of the steps interrelate.

After, be sure to go back and tackle the to-dos step by step.

Finally, make no excuses — you did the hard bit by getting a degree. Now all you need to do is some (relatively) simple exercises, discipline yourself, and put in some dedicated time and effort.

Through reading and enacting the advice contained within *The Career Lab Formula*, **you will land the STEM job you desire.**

The Career Lab Formula

Are you ready to kickstart your STEM career?

STEP 1:
The Biggest Job Searching Secrets That No One Tells You

On average, it can take anywhere between 3 to 6 months to land a position that you love — sometimes even longer.

But don't fret!

The essential thing to remember is that landing a great STEM job is akin to a marathon *(not a sprint!)*.

So, it's best to pace yourself or risk getting burned out. Be kind to yourself during the job application process — burnout will make you far less productive.

A great way to approach the application process is to ***put yourself on a schedule.***

To start, ask yourself the following question:

How much time am I ready to commit to my STEM job search?

There are many things you could do with your time. It could be optimizing your resume, networking, or searching/applying for jobs online.

But how much time should you take? Will you do 1 hour a day, Monday through Friday? 3 hours every week?

Whatever you decide, commit yourself.

And, to keep yourself accountable… **put it in your calendar. This time is non-negotiable!**

In other words — if, on every Tuesday and Thursday from 3-5pm you commit to working on your job search and your best friend calls you and says, *"come to the gym with me at 3 this afternoon,"* then you must answer with a cold, hard *"NO!" (Or, phrase it a little bit nicer, like, "No thank you, friend.")* Tell them that you can meet them at 5:30pm after you've done the work you promised yourself you'd do.

So go ahead — right now — make a commitment to yourself. Put a block on your phone calendar for the hours during the week that you'll work on your search and set a 15min reminder before you have to work.

And do this every week until you find a job.

Do you know what will *really* put you on a schedule? Getting a part-time job.

STEP 1

Yep — you read that right — getting a part-time job can help you land the STEM job of your dreams.

This part-time job could be anything that requires a commitment: working the front desk at a YMCA, bagging groceries, or even volunteering at your local farmer's market.

Why, you may ask?

Well, anything that offers around 10 hours a week will help you maintain your schedule. It could be paid or unpaid. In the context of landing a STEM job, it doesn't really matter. The point here is that you'll have someone who can observe your work and provide feedback so you can improve.

The best way to land a part-time role is to ask around. There are a few methods you can employ. You can:

- Fire off emails to local businesses,
- ask owners of the places where you like to hang out *(like the town's cultural center)* if they need any help, or
- ask friends who work in jobs who could recommend you.

Be honest that you're looking for something part-time, so you still have the flexibility to search for your ideal STEM job.

Now, let's explore a couple of brief anecdotes.

A candidate I once interviewed, Jacklynn (a Master's in Public Health graduate), worked at her mother's advertising agency.

She was tasked with creating a digital filing system for their marketing contacts. Her initiative proved to me that she could tackle any task with a sense of curiosity — and even offer suggestions on how to improve something that to others would seem so mundane.

So, I hired her for an entry-level role focused on vaccine market research.

Another individual I coached, Karan, asked his local library if they needed any help. He ended taking an unpaid role restacking books. The experience provided great context to answer some of the behavioral interview questions he was asked for a Data Scientist role within a large eCommerce organization. Not only that, but his manager at the library provided a glowing reference that helped him land the job.

Here are some further advantages to taking a part-time job while you're focused on searching for a full-time role:

1. – It helps you maintain a schedule.

2. – You gain real-world work experience — this is essential if you've never had a job before.

STEP 1

3. – It helps you enhance your soft-skills. Soft skills are non-technical skills that refer to how you work. Examples of these are: Do you arrive to work on time daily (time management)? Can you carry a task through to the end in a quality and timely manner (project management)? If there are delays, when and how do you tell your boss (effective communication)? How do you handle conflict? If your boss isn't present, can you make high-level decisions (decision making and taking responsibility)? Are you happy doing mundane tasks (positive attitude)?

4. – It shows initiative. You won't spend your whole working life waiting for other people to tell you what to do. When you find problems and solve them yourself, you'll be a much better asset for any company.

5. – It provides a real-world reference beyond your college professors. Don't get me wrong — your professors are great references, but they can only speak to your intellectual understanding or provide context on your technical domain knowledge *(although this is still extremely important)*. However, the manager at your part-time job will be able to tell your future employer what type of employee you are — and this is where your soft skills come into play. You'll learn more about references in STEP 8.

6. – Having a part-time job will keep your mind occupied, and keep you motivated while you hunt down a STEM job. Remember, it can take anywhere between 3 to 6 months to land a full-time position that you like. The last thing you want is to mope around while you search.

So, to recap: Make a schedule and stick to it. Get a part-time job. Stay focused, disciplined, and believe in yourself.

Even if the hunt takes a while, believe me — **with perseverance, you will land that STEM job.**

STEP 2:
The Basics: Creating a Resume and a Cover Letter

Your resume is *(almost always)* a company's first introduction to who you are — and it's a chance for you to tell your story.

But you must make your story engaging, neat, and eye-catching.

Why?

Because unfortunately, recruiters and hiring managers often have to rummage through hundreds of resumes for one position.

Here's a little factoid for you — a 2018 Ladders Inc. Eye-Tracking Study revealed that recruiters skim resumes for an average of 7.4 seconds!

So — you may ask — *how do I get my resume noticed?*

Simple.

Have a well-formatted and concise document that includes the following information, *in this specific order:*

- **Name, phone number, email address.**

- **Link to your LinkedIn profile** – *(*more on this in STEP 3*)* and/or a portfolio or senior project site *(if you have one).*

- **Introduction/Personal Summary** – This is a short summary of who you are and what type of role you're looking for. To craft an outstanding resume introductory statement, you must present — in a intriguing and fascinating manner — the information that the recruiter wants in just a few lines. This is where you should include the buzzwords and skills needed for the role (more on this in STEP 4).

- **Education** – name of the university you attended, year you graduated, and degree you obtained.

- **Bullet point a summary of relevant classes** – This is especially important for STEM graduates who are applying for traditional jobs in their field, but who don't have any relevant work experience. Your future employers will want to know that you have at least been exposed to the content, tools, and technology needed for the Role. For example, if you're applying to be a Technician for a Molecular Biology Lab, did you take a class on DNA, RNA, phospholipids, and proteins? Or common lab techniques used to research the biological activities of these components? Conceptually, do you know what a PCR is and what it's used for?

- ***Bullet point a summary of core competencies.*** Examples of this could be computer programs, lab techniques or industry specific governances that you are experienced with.

- ***Senior Project*** *(if you had one)* – Title of your Senior Project and 2-3 bullet points highlighting the project scope, your role, and what you learned.

- ***Work experience*** – start listing your work experience in reverse chronological order — from newest to oldest. Include the company's name and location, your title, and then 3-4 bullet points reflecting your accomplishments. Also include the actions you took to benefit the company or organization. ***DO NOT*** just write a laundry list of your roles/ responsibilities. Listing out all your responsibilities will make your resume tedious and show a recruiter that you're filling space for the sake of it. Anyone can do a task that's handed to them. What a recruiter wants to know is Did you understand why you were doing the task? What benefit did the company get from the task/did it provide a solution?

- ***Awards/ Publications*** *(if you have any)*. Go ahead, brag about yourself!

- ***Interests/ Hobbies*** – this could help start an interview conversation and even loosen nerves before you get into any typical interview questions. It can also help hiring managers and recruiters build a personal connection at the start of the interview. *(I once had a candidate list that he was the winner of his college's America's Got Talent contest. I was curious to learn more, and it was a fun way to start an interview. And yes — he got the job, a Digital Marketing Manager role at a small Life Science company. His resume already highlighted his technical skills. His interests showcased he was willing to get out of his comfort zone — a critical soft skill as he'd be interacting with Product Managers and Executives to build the company's digital ecosystem.)*

Now you know what content to include in your resume.

But formatting your resume is also essential — and you can use it to set yourself apart from other candidates:

- Your resume should be limited to **_1 page only_**. As you're a recent college graduate, a resume longer than 1 page may signal to a hiring manager that you don't know how to be succinct.

- **_0.5 to 1-inch margins_** on each side – Most hiring managers prefer lots of white space on a resume — it makes them easier to read. *(And*

STEP 2

many hiring managers will use the white space on a printed resume to take notes.)

- **Your resume should be bullet points** – no paragraphs! Make sure to align all bullets/sub bullets.

- Use **parallel sentence structure**. In other words — if, under your Work Experience section, you start the first bullet point with a past tense verb, then start all the subsequent bullets the same way.

Now, just as importantly — there's also information you **should NOT** include on your resume, including:

- **Your address** – all communication will be via phone or email.

- **A photo** - save your photo for your LinkedIn profile.

- **References** - if the company is interested in speaking with your references, they will ask. This request usually comes at the end of an interview process (more on this in STEP 8).

- **Salary expectations** - In some states, it's illegal for a company to ask for your *salary history*. Check your state's employment website for more details. As far as salary expectations are concerned, like references, the company will ask for this information when they need it (more on this in STEP 7).

But what about templates?

There are many resume templates available online — and I encourage you to use one that you like.

But, keep in mind that not all templates are created equal. Make sure you pick something that's visually appealing, offers lots of white space, and is well formatted. When you're adding text, use a 12-point font size, stick to traditional fonts *(like Arial, Calibri, or Times New Roman)*, and majority of the font color should be black — you can use a different color for your name.

Let's look at a real-world example — a couple of resumes from someone who we'll call Charlie Chemistry *(we'll meet Charlie a few times throughout this book)*.

Charlie recently graduated with a bachelor's degree in Chemistry *(get it?!)*

He wants to use his degree to land a full-time position. He has no relevant prior work experience but has worked several part-time jobs throughout college.

Most recently — to stay on a schedule while he hunts for a full-time job — he joined a local hospital, filling room service orders in their cafeteria.

STEP 2

Charlie landed this paid part-time job by asking his high school friends if they knew anyone who needed some help.

(Ah, to have friends who've got your back!)

Anyway, let's review his original resume and then the refined version based on the guidelines we just discussed.

The Career Lab Formula

Charlie Chemistry's <u>Original</u> Resume:

CHARLIE CHEMISTRY

55 Street Name
Town, State 90210

(777)-777-7777
harliechemistry@Outlook.com

- Completion of bachelor's degree in Chemistry from University of Massachusetts Lowell *(May 2018)* • Strong critical thinking/problem solving • Group Coordinator/Team Communication Skills • Occupational Safety and Health Administration (OSHA) • Chemical Hygiene Plan (CHP) • Hazard Communication Standard (HazCom) • Information Retrieval for chemicals/safety • SciFinder experienced • ChemDraw experienced • Molecular Modeling

EDUCATION

University of Massachusetts Lowell
Chemistry, BS

May 2018 Completion

- Responsible Chemist • Organic Chemistry I & II • Organic Chemistry I & II Laboratory • Physical Chemistry I & II • Physical Chemistry I Laboratory • Physical Bioinorganic Lab • Analytical Chemistry I & II • Analytical Chemistry I & II Laboratory • Forensics Chemistry I & II • Forensics Chemistry I Laboratory • Advanced Inorganic Chemistry • Advanced Inorganic Chemistry Laboratory • Biochemistry • Physiological Chemistry I & II • Organic Chemistry • Information Retrieval for Chemist • Biology I

SKILLS AND ABILITIES

Proficient in: Microsoft Words, Microsoft Excel, Microsoft PowerPoint, ChemDraw, Spartan, SciFinder Scholar, Information Retrieval

Instrumental Experience: FT-IR (ATR), Fluorometry, UV-Vis Spectrophotometry, Flame Atomic Absorption Spectroscopy (FAAS), Ion-selective Electrode (ISE), High Performance Liquid Chromatography (HPLC), Gas Chromatography/Mass Spectrometer (GC/MS), Graphite Furnace Atomic Spectroscopy (GFAS), Direct Current Plasma Atomic Emission Spectroscopy (DCP), Raman Spectroscopy, H-NMR, Differential Scanning Calorimetry (DSC)

EMPLOYMENT HISTORY

Chelmsford Stop and Shop
Produce Clerk

January 2012 – August 2013

- Preparation/Organization of stock items • Proper food rotation • Customer Service • Food preparation of salad bar • Proper food hazard waste • Cardboard disposal operator

Mahoney's Gas Station, Lowell
Booth Management

September 2013 – June 2014

- Money management • Computer-based pump system • Independent worker • Customer Service

Lahey Hospital Medical Center Burlington
Nutrition Care Representative

August 2014 – Present

- Preparation/Organization of Patient's items • Delivery to Patient's room • Strong Team Communication Skills • Customer/Patient Assistance *(In Person & Phone)* • Strong Communication Skills with Patients

---

References Available Upon Request

STEP 2

Charlie Chemistry's Revised Resume:

CHARLIE CHEMISTRY

(777) 777-7777 | CHARLIECHEMISTRY@Outlook.com

PROFESSIONAL SUMMARY

Recent Bachelor's of Science in Chemistry graduate with strong work-ethic, looking for a full-time laboratory based research position.

CORE COMPETENCIES

- ✓ Familiar with key analytical tools: FT-IR, Flurometery, UV-Vis Spectrophotometry, FAAS, SE, HPLC, GC/MS, GFAS, DCP, Raman Spectroscopy, H-NMR, DSC
- ✓ Informational Retrieval of Chemical data
- ✓ SciFinder, ChemDraw and Spartan
- ✓ OSHA, CHP and HazCom rules
- ✓ Critical thinking/problem solving
- ✓ Strong interpersonal skills
- ✓ Microsoft Office

EDUCATION

University of Massachusettes Lowell | Bachelor of Science Chemistry   2018

Relevant coursework includes:
Responsible Chemist • Organic Chemistry (I & II) + Lab • Physical Chemistry (I & II) • Physical Chemistry I Lab • Physical Bioinorganic Lab • Analytical Chemistry (I & II) + Lab • Forensics Chemistry (I & II) • Forensics Chemistry I Lab • Advanced Inorganic Chemistry + Lab • Biochemistry • Organic Chemistry • Information Retrieval for Chemist • Biology I

PROFESSIONAL WORK HISTORY

Lahey Hospital Medical Center   Burlington, MA
Nutritional Care Representative   Aug 2014- present
- Responsible for preparation/organization of patient's food items
- Ensured on time delivery to patient's room
- Showcased strong interpersonal skills with patients and staff
- Effectively communicated to confirm accuracy of food and tray preparation

Mahoney Gas Station   Lowell, MA
Booth Management   Sept 2013- June 2014
- Independent worker
- Solely managed computer based-pump system
- Coordinated end-of-day money administration
- Facilitated customer questions with friendliness and courtesy

Stop and Shop   Chelmsford, MA
Produce Clerk   Jan 2012- Aug 2013
- Prepared and organized stock items to guarantee proper food rotation
- Assisted customer service

Consider the differences. What were the major errors in the original version? What formatting mistakes were made in the original version?

Which resume looks better to you? What other changes would you recommend Charlie make to his resume?

Once you've found some answers to these questions, let's move on.

Writing a cover letter

A good rule of thumb is to always write a cover letter. But your cover letter is especially important when you're just starting your career and have limited direct work experience.

While a resume is a more static overview of your education and experience — a cover letter allows you to bring your story to life. You can use one to explain your experiences and even illustrate your personality.

Even if you have a lite resume, an engaging cover letter will give you a leg up.

Your cover letter should include your soft and technical skills and your strengths.

For your soft skills, you don't need to list them out. Instead, use the cover letter to explain how you utilized your soft skills.

STEP 2

As you're a recent college graduate, I'm sure you have a long list of hard *(or technical)* skills in your toolbox. If you've mastered a particular software suite *(like MATLAB or a Cheminformatics software)* — detail your experience. Be sure to explain what you've created, organized, or implemented using these hard skills.

Your cover letter should also showcase your relevant experiences(s). And, even though you're a recent college graduate, you *do* have experience.

Of course, your part-time job is a great example of experience — but there are many more from your personal and college life that you can draw from.

For example, Did you organize and lead your Fraternity's public service day? Did you start a successful online blog or YouTube channel? Did you draw comics for your school newspaper?

If you have a hard time identifying your strengths or relevant experiences, ask your friends, college classmates, former professors, or even your manager from your part-time job. They can give you honest outsiders' input.

Plus, adding these personal and creative touches to your cover letter will help set it apart from the same old boring cover letters that recruiters have to read over and over.

Always end your cover letter by impressing your prospective employer by communicating your dedicated vision and future within the company. You don't need a detailed 5-year plan, but take the time to research the company you are applying for and discuss the impact you would make if you were hired for this role.

Let's say you're applying for a junior level programmer role at a small tech startup. In that case, you might express your interest in learning more about project management in the event of the company's expansion. An employee who's passionate about advancing their career in-house could be extremely attractive to future employers.

Here is an example cover letter template from our friend Charlie Chemistry. I call this a "template" because Charlie will want to add details based on the job description ([more details in STEP 4](#)).

STEP 2

Charlie Chemistry's Cover Letter Template:

Charlie Chemistry
Charlie.chemistry@outlook.com
777-777-7777

Dear R&D Team:

Please accept my resume for *[ABC position]* at *[Company]*. This role would be an ideal first step in my career as I am looking for a challenging laboratory-based Chemistry role within a company who has a strong reputation in the market as well as a culture that values its employees.

I am confident that my core Chemistry coursework as well as my part-time work experience will serve *[Company]* well in this position. For example, my [XYZ] classes, exposed me to the necessary chemistry tools, such as [insert buzz words or hard skills needed to accomplish role].

Additionally, while I was searching for a full-time job that leveraged my degree, I decided to take a part-time role as Nutritional Care Representative at Lahey Hospital. In this role, I leveraged my time management, personal and communication skills to help achieve the departments goal of ensuring on-time and accurate delivery of food service orders to patients. Although this position is beyond the scope of my degree, I trust it showcased my proactive initiative and willingness to learn new soft skills such as *[insert 3 soft skills based on job description]*

I look forward to discussing employment possibilities with you.

Thank you for your time.

Sincerely,

Charlie Chemistry

Was Charlie able to use his Cover Letter to bring his resume to life? Is there anything missing from Charlie's Cover Letter template? What other changes would you recommend Charlie make to his Cover Letter template?

You have skills. Now, use your cover letter to show it.

Once you've completed your resume and cover letter, ask someone to review your documents for flow, clarity, spelling, and grammatical errors.

These will now be your "Master Resume" and "Template Cover Letter." I use these terms because **you must tailor your resume and cover letter for <u>every</u> job application.**

I'm not talking about a complete overhaul, but you should tweak your resume and cover letter to align with each specific job and company.

Tweaking may mean comparing your resume to the job description and adding a few phrases or buzzwords to your bullet points, so you hit all the keywords a company is looking for. *(Make sure this sounds organic, though — don't just insert out-of-context buzzwords everywhere.)*

Ensuring you use buzzwords is especially important if you're applying for jobs in large organizations (think GE, Apple, or Amgen).

These companies use algorithms to scan resumes.

STEP 2

In other words, even if you're the perfect fit for the job, it's likely that not having those buzzwords will get your resume put in the "no thank you" pile before a human even reads it.

Even for smaller companies, the hiring manager will want to see that you read the job description and wrote your resume to make it relevant for the role.

Yes, this means spending more time before applying — but it'll benefit you in the long run.

[In STEP 4](), we'll review how to read a job description to know which phrases/buzzwords to include.

So, to recap: Create a concise, well-formatted resume that highlights your accomplishments and the positive impact your actions had on the work you were doing. A cover letter is a must as it helps to humanize your resume by bringing your experiences and personality to life.

Make sure to tailor these documents to the specific job you're applying for.

Now that you have your resume and cover letter completed, you're in a perfect position to let the world know on LinkedIn…

STEP 3:
Creating a LinkedIn Profile (and Thoughts About Other Social Media Platforms)

You may be wondering, *What's LinkedIn? (or you may know what it is already, but bear with me.)*

Simply put, LinkedIn is an online professional social network with *(at the time of writing)* almost 700 million users.

Pay attention to it because it's the platform for the future of hiring — and most recruiters use LinkedIn to source candidates.

While Instagram, Facebook, and TikTok are your personal social networks, LinkedIn is where you can interact with people you've worked with, want to work with, or might want to know professionally *(like alumni)*.

LinkedIn is the best online place to document all your professional experiences, education, and coursework you've completed. It's also where you should document the expertise you've gained in your extracurricular activities in a visually appealing and dynamic format.

(Tip: Don't use LinkedIn like other social networking platforms and just connect with all your buddies.)

Additionally, you can browse job postings, read work-related articles, post your own insights, and connect with recruiters.

You can also use LinkedIn to find people for Informational Interviews ([more on this in STEP 5)](#), keep up to date with companies you admire, or stay in touch with the network you've acquired so far.

LinkedIn is also a great way to build an online brand. Often, hiring managers and recruiters will Google you if your resume piques their interest.

Your LinkedIn profile should be one of the first search results that pop up.

But, to make sure — take a break right now to check. Go to Google and search your full name.

What comes up? Is there anything you wouldn't want your future employer to see? Perhaps some late-night partying pictures on Instagram?

Now go into all of your other social networking accounts and set them to "private."

STEP 3

You may even need to contact your college chess club to get that embarrassing picture of you dressed as a pirate and taking a tequila shot pulled from their website.

So, how do you create a LinkedIn profile?

Well, the good news is that the platform is extremely user-friendly and intuitive.

Also — once you've finished resume-building — your LinkedIn profile will take no time at all because you can copy and paste stuff over.

Here are the basics of a LinkedIn profile:

- Add a ***headshot photo***. You don't need to spend money to have a professional take your picture. Do your hair, put on an outfit that you'd wear to a job interview (men: suit jacket, plain collar shirt, and tie; ladies: blazer, plain blouse, simple jewelry, and minimal makeup).

  Now, grab your cellphone and your mom *(or anyone else who's willing to help)*. Have her take the picture in an area that has good lighting *(or go outside where there is natural lighting)* and make sure nothing's in the background.

  This is just a headshot, so make sure the picture is taken from your shoulders up. *(Oh, and **remember to smile**. It makes you appear more approachable.)*

Once you have some photos taken, upload the best one to your LinkedIn profile.

By adding a photo, you give people visiting your LinkedIn profile a multifaceted perception of who you are. You're no longer just another anonymous applicant — you're a friendly face.

- Add a killer ***headline and summary***. Your summary section is another opportunity to add personality to your profile and help you leave a memorable impression on recruiters. Focus on selling yourself, particularly the traits that make you unique and help you stand out from others.

    Answer some of the following questions:

    Who are you? What are you excited and passionate about? What is your long-term goal and why?

    By focusing on writing a purpose-based summary *(i.e., what you'd bring to a team or company if you got hired)*, you'll attract more attention from recruiters and hiring managers — but keep it short.

- Next, put ***keywords*** and/or your ***core competencies*** into your summary. Since many recruiters use LinkedIn for its search function, use keywords to make it easy for recruiters to find you. A great way to identify keywords to use in your summary is to look at job descriptions and find patterns or repeating words. (Similar to the introduction section in your resume.) What in-demand skills do you have?

- The rest of your LinkedIn profile can just be an easy copy-paste of your **education details and even your work experience** from your resume. Especially if you've done a great job on your resume summarizing your work experience in 3-4 punchy bullet points, then there's no need to create more work for yourself. Copy and paste away!

Let's look at our friend Charlie Chemistry's LinkedIn profile:

Charlie's Headline reads: *Recent Bachelor of Science in Chemistry graduate with strong work ethic, looking for a full-time laboratory research or chemical manufacturing position in the greater Boston area.*

Charlie's Summary and Keyword in his About Section: *Recent Bachelor's of Science in Chemistry graduate with strong work ethic, looking for a full-time laboratory research or chemical manufacturing position.*

Core Competencies:

- *Familiar with key analytical tools: FT-IR, Fluorometry, UV-Vis Spectrophotometry, FAAS, SE, HPLC, GC/MS, GFAS, DCP, Raman Spectroscopy, H-NMR, and DSC*

- *Informational Retrieval of Chemical data*
- *SciFinder, ChemDraw, and Spartan*
- *OSHA, CHP, and HazCom rules*
- *Strong critical thinking/problem-solving skills*
- *Strong interpersonal skills*
- *Microsoft Office*

The rest of Charlie's LinkedIn profile is just a copy/paste of his experiences from his resume.

However, Charlie did make 1 extra addition to his LinkedIn profile that didn't appear on his resume. Under the Education section, Charlie added the title and a PDF of the poster from his Senior Thesis — a great way for him to show off his work!

So, to recap: LinkedIn is a big deal because it's the platform for the future of hiring. Not having a LinkedIn profile almost means you don't exist in the working world.

Remember to Google search yourself and set all your other social media platforms to private.

STEP 4:
The Job Search Itself

Ah, finally. The moment you've been waiting for — the actual job search!

Let's get down to business. In this STEP, we'll cover:

- Where you should look for a job
- How to set alerts
- What search terms to use
- What can you actually do with your degree, and
- How to read a job description.

Before we get into all these details, I need you to do one thing — ***get yourself organized.***

I know it probably feels like it's time for you to start the job search — and you likely want to hit the ground running at full speed.

But I promise you that — by organizing your hunt — you'll drastically increase your chances of job-landing success.

Know that you may end up applying to 5-10 jobs a week. Therefore, I advise you keep track of where you apply.

If you don't — and the hiring manager or human resources business partner from a company calls you to set up an interview — I guarantee that your memory won't serve you.

(Do you want to risk creating a bad first impression by seeming unprepared?)

The simplest way to keep track of all your applications is to create an Excel file. Go ahead and create one with the following columns:

- Date of application
- Company name
- Company location
- Hyperlink to job description
- Networking/ contacts *(if any)*

Now, every time you apply for a job, log the relevant information into your spreadsheet.

Okay — you're now ready to browse for jobs.

Let's start with some good news — you don't need to search the website of every company you're interested in working for.

STEP 4

There are a few key sites I recommend you look at as they serve as search engines that scout company job boards.

The best part? They're free!

Let's explore some of these sites.

Indeed.com: Indeed posts listings for job seekers in every industry and at every level — from entry to executive. Candidates can filter and search by job title, location, date posted, and experience level. Indeed is 100% free and you don't need to sign up for an account. However, having an account will allow you to receive email alerts when new jobs are posted, upload your resume to complete applications more quickly, and receive messages from recruiters and prospective employers. The best part? It's simple — Indeed's interface is highly intuitive and designed to make your job search move faster.

Monster.com: Like Indeed, Monster caters to job seekers from all experience levels. You need to create an account using your email address to apply to any job listing on Monster, but it's easy to set up.

LinkedIn.com: LinkedIn is also a great site for job hunting. Unlike Indeed and Monster that serve as search engines for company job boards, many companies post specific jobs directly to LinkedIn. Additionally, LinkedIn allows you to add recruiters to your virtual network, making it the best website for connecting with them directly.

The 3 sites listed will cover close to 90% of all available jobs. However, there are some other sites that you may also be interested in — your college job board and industry specific sites like massbio.org or biospace.org for pharma/biotech jobs, for example.

For LinkedIn, Indeed, and Monster, you can set email alerts for jobs in your field, specific companies, desired geographic location, salary range, and more using most search engines, job boards, and career sites.

This way, you can be the first person to know when your ideal job has been posted.

For entry level roles, there are a handful of job titles that'll help you discover the right roles for recent graduates. Here are a few examples that'll serve as a good starting point to set up alerts:

- Entry level
- Analyst
- Associate
- Technician
- Specialist
- Coordinator

As for additional search terms beyond the job title — they can be endless and depend on the type of role you're searching for. For example, it could be

STEP 4

"chemistry lab coordinator" or "associate process engineer."

Now that you've got yourself organized and know what sites to use for your job hunt, let's take a minute to discuss the types of jobs you should apply for and address a question that I'm asked frequently — *What can I do with my degree?*

The advantage of having a STEM degree is that it demonstrates you're highly analytical and logical. These skills are needed for a variety of industries and roles — and some of these are non-traditional and may not be front of mind for you.

Examples of non-traditional STEM jobs that spring to mind are:

- Statistical Analyst for an Investment Bank,
- Associate Consultant at a Management Consulting firm *(that's where I got my start),*
- Technology Analyst for a Venture Capital firm that focuses on emerging tech start-ups,
- Market Research Coordinator for a Life Science company,
- QA/QC analyst for a Medical Device company,
- Sales Representative for a Green Energy Company, or even

- Analyst for the CIA *(someone I know who graduated with a biology degree started their career here)*.

Don't see the job you're considering listed above? No worries. In the APPENDIX, you'll find a plethora of sample industries that are potentially relevant based on your area of study.

Another way to identify what jobs you could apply for is to find out what your university's alumni are doing.

One way to do this is to search on LinkedIn for folks who recently graduated from your college *(within the past 2-3 years)* with a similar degree to you, and find the answers to the following questions:

- What company are they working for?
- What is their title?
- What did they do after college to help position them to get the degree?

While you are exploring their profile, consider sending them a quick message and ask them if they're open to an Informational Interview (more on that in STEP 5).

How to read a job posting:

A job description provides a good initial overview of a role and company.

STEP 4

Learning how to read them correctly will help you nail an application or interview or help you decide if the role is not for you.

The majority of job postings will have 4 main components:

1. **Company Description:** As you've probably worked out already, this describes the company, their values, and what they prioritize. This is a great way to get an overview of the company. However, be sure to also do your own research to get a more rounded impression of what they're like and how they operate. Also, pay close attention to phrases like "our core values." Why? Because if you land an interview at any company, you'll likely be asked about how your working style aligns with their company values. Make sure you're prepared to tell the interviewer how you think you'll fit in at the company.

2. **Role Description:** this section tells you about the job itself and what the hiring manager expects out of the position. When you're interviewing, use this role description to your advantage and align your responses with what the company is looking for — this will help paint you as a great match for the role! This is also a great place to scout for keywords or industry specific terminology to include in your resume.

3. **Responsibilities:** this is everything in the role that you'll be responsible for *(in other words, what your role entails)*. And it's the cornerstone of any job posting, so focus on this as you tailor your cover letter and resume for the role. Most importantly — as you read the responsibilities section — ask yourself, *"Have I done this before?"* If so, make sure you highlight that in your cover letter and resume, and bring it up during the interview. However, also ask yourself, *"Do I want to do this?"* **If the answer is no, then don't apply.** We spend a significant chunk of our lives at work — why would you want to end up in a role you wouldn't enjoy?

4. **Qualifications:** essentially, these are the skills needed to complete the work as described in the responsibilities section. Sometimes, job listings provide both minimum and preferred qualifications. You should have 80% of the minimum skills. A word of caution here — since you're applying for entry-level roles — **make sure that the role requires at minimum a 4-year college degree.** I've met too many people who apply for hourly/ labor jobs *(especially on the manufacturing side)* where the minimum educational requirement is a high school diploma. Trust me, this is not the right job for you! Sure, these types of jobs might help you get your foot in the door, but you'll likely get bored or not have the necessary visibility or training to get you to other roles in the organization.

STEP 4

Before we go any further, let's revisit our job-hunting buddy, Charlie Chemistry.

Charlie logged onto Indeed and did a simple search of "entry level chemistry" jobs in "Boston, MA."

Here are some examples of hypothetical job descriptions that came up:

Associate Scientist I - Boston, MA (Entry Level)

ABC ANALYTICAL Life Sciences
City, State 01801

Job details: Full-time

Full Job Description
Summary
We are seeking a talented and self-motivated scientist (recent graduate or upcoming graduate) who is eager to be part of our success, and who embraces our core values: Integrity, Excellence, and Teamwork. This role requires scientific curiosity, willingness and eagerness to learn and support drug development efforts. If you have a passion for hands-on problem solving to develop cutting-edge pharmaceuticals, this is the job for you! Working in a dynamic, fast-paced, team-oriented and collaborative environment at ABC ANALYTICAL Life Sciences! **Local candidates only please.**

Responsibilities include:

- Help support planning, execution and reporting on analytical or formulation development experiments.
- Sample preparation for and operation of a variety of analytical instruments including HPLC, CE, UV, & Dissolution Apparatus.
- Support the analysis and interpretation of complex scientific data.
- Preparation of client update presentations, technical reports, and protocols.
- Identify and propose solutions for technical problems.
- Gain proficiency and technical expertise with one or two laboratory instruments.
- Carry out other scientific and laboratory duties as required.

Required background and experience includes:

- Recent Bachelor's degree in chemistry, biochemistry, or related field.
- Preference to a candidate with internship or coop experience in industry or academic laboratory experience related to drug development.
- The ability to read and understand relevant scientific literature, procedures, and protocols.
- Preference to experience in laboratory or internship with analytical and processing equipment and laboratory operations is a plus.
- Exceptional written and verbal communication and problem-solving abilities.
- Strong organizational, documentation and time management skills.

Required Knowledge and Skills

- Fundamental understanding of principles, practices and techniques of chemistry/biochemistry.
- Willingness to learn and understand of operation and routine maintenance of scientific analytical equipment, including but not limited to HPLC, UV, CE, DLS.
- Motivated to become familiar with techniques to analyze small molecule and/or biologic pharmaceuticals, including but not limited to dissolution, lyophilization, CD, CE, DSC, DLS, TGA, XRPD, LC-MS.
- Proficiency in Microsoft Word, Excel and PowerPoint.
- Effective written and verbal communicator.
- Contribute and help support the accomplishment of team or work unit goals, objectives and activities.
- Establish and maintain effective working relationships with a variety of individuals.

Based on the **Required Background** in the job description, I'd say that Charlie's a good candidate for this role: he has a recent Bachelor's degree in Chemistry, his resume lists exposure to lab analytical tools like HPLC, and his part-time job proves he has experience in soft skills like communication and time management.

The job description has multiple repeated keywords throughout: "analytical techniques," "problem solving abilities," "team oriented/ collaborative/ effective working relationships," "exceptional communication skills," and "effective communicator."

Also, in the Summary, the company discusses their **core values**.

Charlie should mention all the keywords and how his core values align in the cover letter. If he gets called for an interview, I wouldn't be surprised if these are the areas where he gets asked technical questions — but also behavioral and fit questions regarding the company's core values and team-oriented culture (more on this in STEP 6).

STEP 4

Here's another hypothetical job description that showed up for a consulting role:

Research Associate, Consulting- job post

ACME Research Inc, Boston, MA 02110; Job details: Job Type, Full-time

Full Job Description

ACME Research is actively looking for smart, scientifically minded individuals who are looking to explore employment opportunities outside of a lab or engineering setting! This position is a great entry level opportunity for candidates looking to use their sciences or engineering education in a business setting by working on consulting projects in an advisory services firm.

Research Associates learn and perform a variety of skill sets including researching technologies and markets, analyzing companies, constructing landscapes of innovation in emerging technologies, assessing market opportunities for new technologies, and conducting technical interviews with executives in order to help our clients make better decisions about R&D investments, partnerships, and technology strategy.

We are specifically seeking a Research Associate for our Consulting practice, so you must enjoy and thrive in an intense, deadline driven, multi-tasking, problem solving environment with diverse personalities across a geographically dispersed team.

Job Responsibilities

- Conduct primary and extensive secondary research on emerging technology topics drawing on diverse sources, including business and trade press articles, scientific publications, patent filings, and conference presentations.
- Create data containers and frameworks for the collection and ranking of technologies and companies.
- Analyze, rank, and prioritize technologies and companies along logic-driven rulesets.
- Execute interviews and briefings with senior executives at innovative companies as well as leaders of cutting-edge university and government labs.
- Contribute to technical and executive level MS PowerPoint deliverables and presentations.

Qualifications and Skills

- Given the highly technical focus of our work and our clients' work, a degree in the sciences and/or engineering fields is required, Chemical or Bioengineering, Chemistry, Biochemistry, Physics
- Any prior work experience in a technical/analytical setting is a plus.
- Strong organizational skills and attention to detail; exhibits logical thought, communication, planning, and action in accomplishing multi-step tasks.
- Likes and enjoys multitasking and working on multiple subject areas.
- Deep intellectual curiosity and desire to learn about emerging technologies and their impact.
- Willingness to do what it takes to meet client needs in a fast paced, client oriented and deadline driven environment; possessing an entrepreneurial, enthusiastic, collegial, and collaborative approach to work is essential to success.
- Excellent office software skills.

More About ACME Research:

ACME Research is a leading provider of tech-enabled research and advisory solutions, helping clients drive growth through technology innovation. A pioneer in the research industry, ACME uniquely combines technical expertise and business insights with a proprietary intelligence platform, using advanced analytics and data science to surface true leading indicators. With quality data derived from primary research, fact-based analysis, and opinions that challenge traditional thinking, ACME clients are empowered to make more informed decisions today to ensure future success.

Based on this job description, I'd say that anyone with a STEM degree *(including Charlie)* is a good candidate for Research Associate Consulting role, especially if they want to learn the business side of STEM.

This job description also has multiple keywords that are repeated throughout: "technical/ analytical," "intellectual curiosity," "fast-paced," "intense," and "problem solving."

This type of language is typical for consulting roles as you often work long hours *(and even weekends)*.

However, once you build a strong business acumen, this will provide a great platform for ascending to higher level roles within the industry.

Here, the key question for Charlie is whether he wants to do this type of work.

If he does, then he can follow the same cover letter and interview guidance outlined for any other job.

If he doesn't, then I'd recommend he looks elsewhere without applying.

Alternatively, if Charlie is unsure, he can choose to connect with someone on LinkedIn who works at ACME research to schedule an informational interview to find out more about what the day-to-day is like as a Research Associate at this company.

STEP 4

So, my advice to you is… **be more like Charlie!** Look carefully at job descriptions and make sure you only apply to jobs you will actually enjoy.

A side note on Contracting jobs:

A Contract job is a non-permanent role within a company. You could be hired by the company directly or through a staffing agency *(example: Kelly Scientific)*.

In either case, these are short-term positions that can last anywhere from 3 months to a year.

Some contract roles are full-time, others are part-time — it all depends on the company's needs.

There are many reasons why company's look for contract workers. It may be that they have a special project where they need some short-term support, or perhaps they're looking to fill an immediate need *(like if someone had to go on medical leave or they have a staff shortage for a specific project)*, but don't have the budget to hire someone permanent just yet.

There are advantages to taking a contract role: you gain experience to enhance your resume, you get to test-drive a company's culture/role and — if you do well — there's a chance that the company could offer you a permanent position at the end of your contract.

The downside is that you don't have job security, you won't receive any benefits *(like medical, paid time off, or tuition reimbursement, etc.)* and it's likely you'll be working M-F, 9-5, so you won't have as much time to search for a permeant role.

If you've been hard at work job searching for at least 3 months with no bites, then it doesn't hurt to apply for contract roles just to get some experience.

This is exactly what my nephew Razaad did.

After searching for a permanent full-time job for almost a year — and having many interviews with no offers in hand — he decided to quit his part-time job and take a full-time 8-month contract in a Quality Assurance (QA) Technician role at a small medical device company.

Nevertheless, he was still dedicated to landing a permanent position. So, Razaad continued his job search on evenings and weekends.

The contract role helped him gain real world experience and enhance his soft skills — all of which provided great talking points during the interview process for his permanent role at the diagnostic company.

However, Razaad also learned that he didn't like QA testing and the medical device industry wasn't a place where he could leverage his chemistry degree.

STEP 4

Thus, he was now able to focus his search for roles and industries that were better aligned with his long-term career vision.

So, to recap: Finding the right jobs to apply for means knowing where to search, what keywords to use, and how to read a job description. Make sure you use these keywords in your cover letter, resume, and interview. And be open to exploring Contract roles.

STEP 5:
Networking and Asking For an Informational Interview

Wow, we're halfway through our Journey!

Congrats on making it this far. Let's celebrate all that you've accomplished in the past few months *(or weeks)*! All your hard work up to now will set you up for success for the final 4 steps in this journey.

I'm so happy and excited for you!

We're going to talk about something more fun in this step — networking and asking for informational interviews.

Let's start by exploring the 3 different types of networking:

1. Networking with someone you admire to learn more about their career.

2. Networking with someone at a specific company to learn more about the organizational culture. *(This works well after you've applied for a role at a specific company.)*

3. Networking with recruiters so they can scout and present jobs to you.

The good news is that you can use LinkedIn for all 3 of the networking types above.

Let's get into more detail.

Networking with someone you admire. On LinkedIn, you should've already been connecting with Alumni and/or folks who are in roles that you might be interested in having one day. Once you've made the connection, the next step is to ask for an informational interview.

The key thing to remember during an informational interview is that you're not asking them for a job.

Rather, you're trying to set up a phone call or virtual coffee date to discuss with them their work and gather insights about what it took to get them to where they are now.

The more you learn about the work, the more you'll know whether it's right for you — and you'll also better understand how to follow in their footsteps and land a job.

STEP 5

I know this may sound weird to reach out to someone who you've never met before to ask them about their job or company, but trust me — it's common in today's world.

Once you've researched the person, draft a list of questions you want to ask.

Here are some examples:

- How did you get your current position?
- What was your first job out of college and how did you get it?
- Can you offer me some advice as I look to start my career?

Let's look at a sample message that our friend Charlie Chemistry could use to network with someone he admires via LinkedIn:

Hi [NAME],

I hope this message finds you well. My name is Charlie Chemistry and I'm reaching out because I've read up on your career and the work you've done at Dupont Chemicals, specifically on your research on continuous processing of APIs. I would love the opportunity to learn more from you. Would you be willing to schedule a quick 20-minute phone call to discuss your work, career, and some general insights into the Chemical Manufacturing industry?

If so, do you have availability over the next few weeks? I'm available to speak by phone at the following times in the next two weeks: Mondays and Thursdays from 9am to 1pm or Fridays from noon to 5pm.

Please let me know if one of those dates and times works for you and a good number to reach you at, and I'll send a calendar invite!

Thank you for taking the time to read this message. I hope to speak to you soon!

Many thanks,

Charlie Chemistry
charliechemistry@outlook.com
777-777-7777

Networking with someone at a specific company.
Another way to network after you apply for a job is to do a quick LinkedIn search through your network. Pay attention to whoever you know (or someone who's in contact with someone you want to know) that works at the desired company.

Know that many companies offer a referral bonus, so folks are generally happy to make the connection and perhaps personally recommend you.

Once you've researched the person, draft a list of questions you want to ask. Some examples include:

STEP 5

- ○ What do you know about this role/ team in the company?

- ○ How do you like working at the company?

- ○ What type of training programs does the company offer?

- ○ What are the company's core values?

- ○ Do you know the hiring manager and would you be comfortable sending my resume directly to them?

Let's look at a sample message that Charlie Chemistry could use to network with someone at a specific company for a role that he has applied for *(again using LinkedIn)*:

Hi [NAME],

I hope this message finds you well. My name is Charlie Chemistry and I've recently applied for an Associate Chemist role in the Green Solvents Research & Development team at MilliporeSigma (Requisition #54318F).

As you're a current employee, I was hoping to learn more about the company and the R&D team. Would you be willing to hop on the phone for 20 minutes to discuss MilliporeSigma's core values and the training programs/ resources for individuals who are early in their career?

Do you have availability over the next few weeks? I am available to speak by phone at the following times in the next two weeks: Mondays and Thursdays from 9am to 1pm or Fridays from noon to 5pm..

Please let me know if one of those dates and times works for you and a good number to reach you at, and I'll send a calendar invite!

Thank you for taking the time to read this message. I hope to speak to you soon!

Many thanks,

Charlie Chemistry
charliechemistry@outlook.com
777-777-7777

Networking with recruiters. The good news about networking with recruiters is that you don't have to find them — they'll find you!

Yup, it's their job to connect with new talent, so as long as you have your LinkedIn profile headline set up properly, they'll connect with you.

Don't hesitate to connect with as many recruiters that reach out. Most likely — once they establish a connection — they'll set up a quick call to learn more about you and then ask for a copy of your resume to send along to companies where open positions are available. These positions will unlikely be posted on the company's website, so you don't need to worry about double applying for a role.

Generally, companies will outsource roles to external recruiters if they don't have the necessary in-house resources. So, to entice external recruiters, they'll carve out a handful of roles that are exclusive to that recruiting agency.

For any of the 3 networking types above — once you've made the connection — **make sure to be polite** (and <u>never</u> be pushy).

After you have a phone call with anyone, **always send a follow up thank you note within 24 hours.** Showing appreciation will strengthen the connection, make the person you spoke to feel good, and motivate them to be more willing to speak with you if you reach out to them again in the future.

So, to recap: Networking is a great way to connect with people whom you worked with in the past, who went to your school, and even ***those*** who you admire. Each connection provides you with an opportunity to learn more ***about*** their career path. Remember to always be polite and value the time others are offering you with some well thought out questions — and **always be sure to thank them.**

STEP 6:
Prepping For Interviews (Phone, In-Person, and Virtual)

Interviews can seem scary, and it's perfectly natural to feel intimidated by them.

But there's something you must know that many people don't realize — ***interviews are a 2-way street.***

What do I mean by this?

Well, you're interviewing the company/ team/ hiring manager just as much as they're interviewing you.

Sure, the company's interviewing you to find out if you're a good candidate for the role. However, you can also ask them questions to see if the role and company are right for you, too.

When you're job hunting, there are two types of interviews you need to prepare for:

Phone interview

In-person or virtual interview(s)

Each of these have different expectations and people who you'd be speaking with.

Let's explore these further.

Phone Interviews:

Every job opportunity starts with a phone interview. Most likely, you'll get an email from a Recruiter or a Human Resources Business Partner to set up a phone interview.

Do a quick LinkedIn search to figure out what their role is at the company. Most often, it'll be a member of the recruiting team, which means it *won't* be your potential boss.

What this means is that — during the phone interview — they'll want to tell you more about the position and ask you some basic questions about your work history and why you're interested in this role. Keep that in mind as you prepare answers to potential interview questions.

You'll meet the hiring manager during the in-person interview — where you'll be asked the more difficult interview questions.

After the phone interview with the recruiter, write to them about scheduling the next phase ASAP.

STEP 6

Remember — ***Always proofread your response.*** You're not going to impress anyone if your email or message is full of errors.

If you've applied for multiple roles at a single company, it's okay to be honest — feel free to ask the emailer to clarify what specific role you're a candidate for.

Understanding which role they're asking you to potentially fill is essential.

Why?

Because then you can go back to the job description to remind yourself of the role, associated responsibilities, and any other details about the company. Of course, your Excel file should make this easy to accomplish!

Read through the job description carefully and focus on keywords that pop up frequently, or the key skills needed for the role. Just like in your resume and cover letter, these are the elements you should try to touch on during your interviews — both telephone and in-person. If it helps, write them down and have them as reference during your interview.

Next, start researching the company. You can do this by visiting the company's website, finding out the major products they sell, reading through their recent press releases, mission, company culture, and then finding answers to related questions *(for example, did they launch a major new product? Just acquire a new company? Who's their CEO?).*

LinkedIn is another great resource to look up company details. The more information you can collect, the better. Ultimately, this step is to ensure that you have a great answer to the question: *"Why are you interested in working for us?"*

Next, prepare by coming up with answers to some typical phone interview questions *(and practice these answers).*

You should be able to answer any technical question or key skills that are required for the role.

Let's look at an example.

In STEP 4, we reviewed an Associate Scientist job description.

If Charlie Chemistry was being interviewed for that role, he should be able to speak about HPLC and UV technologies and how he's used them before. He should also be prepared to answer what he liked or didn't like about these analytical techniques.

Other typical phone interview questions include:

- **Can you tell me more about yourself and background?**
  This is your pitch. Craft an introduction that's brief and to the point. This is an

extremely common first interview question as it really helps the interviewer understand how you communicate. Are you linear, concise, and direct? Are you entertaining? Do you go off on tangents?

Here's an example of Charlie Chemistry's pitch for the Associate Scientist I role:

> *"I recently graduated with a BS in Chemistry from University of Massachusetts Lowell — go River Hawks!*
>
> *I am now looking for a full-time role that leverages my degrees, especially my coursework in analytical methodologies. It was one of my favorite parts of being a Chemistry major. Even my senior thesis leveraged multiple analytical techniques to characterize ferrocenes. So, I am excited to be here today and learn more about the role, the team, and the company."*

- ***Can you walk me through your resume?*** Similar to your pitch, you want to highlight what's most relevant on your resume and how/ why you'd be a good fit for the role.

- ***What do you know about the company?*** Here's a chance to demonstrate your genuine desire for the role, and to show off your research skills!

- ***Tell me about [x] in your resume.*** This is why you should always be truthful on your resume. You must be able to back up what you wrote on there.

- **What interests you about this role?** Or, Why would you be a good candidate for this role? For both of these questions, leverage the buzzwords and skills mentioned in the job description.

- **Where do you see yourself in five years?** There is no right answer to this question, so just tell the truth. If you know where you want to be, discuss it and highlight that this role is a steppingstone to help you achieve your 5-year plan. If you don't, then it's okay to be honest:

  > *"I'm not sure. Right now, I'm eager to learn more about this role, but being in a large organization like this, I'm sure there will be countless opportunities for me to grow."*

- **Are you willing to relocate?** (If you're applying to a job in another city.) And, i**f we don't provide relocation assistance, are you still willing to move?** You should have this figured out before you even interview for the role. If your answer is "no," then be polite and don't waste anyone's time. If your answer is "yes" then tell them your preliminary plans —

  > *"My cousin lives in the same city, and we have discussed plans to potentially room together. So, it this is the right fit for both me and the company, then I'm willing to make the move on my own."*

STEP 6

- **What are your salary requirements?** For now, a perfectly acceptable response is

  "I'm sure you're competitive with market, but right now, I'm more interested in learning about the role and company."

  When it comes to an in-person interview, we'll review sites to reference to determine an appropriate salary range for the role (more on this in STEP 7).

- **How far along are you in your search?** Or, **Are you speaking to other companies?** This is another question that you can answer vaguely —

  "I'm early in my search, so I'm looking at a similar roles at multiple companies."

  However, if you're in multiple late-stage interviews or you have an offer in hand, don't be shy about letting the interviewer know. If the HR recruiter thinks you're a good fit for their role, then they may be able to expedite the hiring process and have you meet key interviewers quickly. It also puts you in a strong position to negotiate for a better salary (more on that in STEP 7).

- **What questions do you have for me?** This last question is important. You should have a few questions ready to ask the interviewer:

  - Why is this role open?

- When are you looking for someone to start?
- What are the next stages in the interview process?
- How large is the team?
- What are the typical working hours for this team?
- What training resources does the company provide?

A typical phone interview takes about 30-45 minutes. You'll need to plan on being somewhere quiet. Be sure to use headphones to block out background noise, and have a microphone that works well if you are called on your computer. Have the job description and your resume pulled up on your laptop. You may even want to have your buzzword/skills cheat sheet handy.

Phone interviews can be intimidating because you can't see the other person's facial expressions and physical cues. My recommendation here is to smile as you answer the questions. Smiling will help you speak more confidently, and confidence is a great trait that'll help you land a job.

Remember to speak slowly, answer professionally, and let the interviewer interrupt you — they may want you to clarify something or go a little deeper in a specific area of your response.

STEP 6

End the call by thanking the interviewer for their time, tell them that you're excited about the role, and that you hope to hear from them soon regarding next steps.

Lastly, send a follow-up thank you email.

Prepping for in-person/ virtual interview (s)

If the phone interview goes well, you'll most likely get a follow-up email from the company inviting you to meet the team for an in-person interview.

Again, reply promptly with the days/ times you're available. If they haven't provided this in the initial email, make sure you ask for a schedule for the day with names of the people you'll be interviewing with.

Similar to phone interviews, your first step will be to do your research. For the individuals you'll be meeting, browse their LinkedIn profiles.

Find out answers to questions like, Where did they pursue their undergraduate degree? What is their current role in the organization? These will indicate the type of questions they'll ask you during interviews. Also, take another look at the company website for any updates or new press releases.

For the in-person interview, I recommend doing a quick online search to find out what the salary range is for the role.

It's likely that you'll be asked about salary expectations again during in-person interviews, so you should have a ~$10K range in mind (see STEP 7 for details).

Next, practice some interview questions or line up mock interviews with family or friends.

I'm sure that you'll be able to nail the technical questions. The harder questions to prepare for are the soft skill, cultural fit, and behavioral ones. I recommend creating 2-3 "brag stories" to help you answer these questions.

The three elements of a brag story are:

1. **Challenge** or situation when you began the project or task.

2. **Action** you took to create a result or solve a problem.

3. **Result** that followed *(if you can quantify the result- even better!)*.

This 3-prong approach is a good way to answer behavioral/culture fit questions that are likely to come up during the in-person interview.

Besides the ones I listed in the phone interview section, here are a few additional questions that may come up during your in-person interview:

- ***What are your biggest strengths?*** This is a good opportunity to brag about what you're good at — 3 adjectives are sufficient. Some strong adjectives that come to mind are: analytical, collaborative, fast-learner, approachable, patient, disciplined, creative. Whatever adjectives you pick, just make sure you can back it up and contextualize it with examples, preferably from your brag stories.

- ***What are your biggest weaknesses?*** The best thing to do here is to say how you're currently developing the weaknesses, and that you'd also use the role to further develop them.

- ***Describe a failure in your academic life.*** You'll be asked this question to determine how you approach and overcome problems. This can also illustrate your ability to take responsibility, bounce back, and refocus after problems occur. To answer this question well, make sure you have your best failure ready and the step-by-step recourse that you followed afterwards. Again, follow the brag story framework. How did this failure inform how you moved forward?

- ***What do you like to do for fun?*** This question can determine a cultural fit within the company and tell them more about what sort of candidate you are. The best way to prepare for these sorts of questions is to do your research thoroughly on the company culture, either through their website, networking, or reading reviews on sites like glassdoor.com.

- ***Tell me about why you chose to go to [XYZ] university and why you decided to major in [ABC] subject.*** How to answer this style of question: Know your personal pitch and how to tell your story well. That includes being able to talk about key decisions you've made and their outcomes. Believe it or not, this is considered a type of public speaking. How well you articulate your background will be essential. You can practice this pitch beforehand —which will elevate your confidence and increase your chances of getting to that all-important next stage.

- ***Give me an example of a time when you solved an analytically difficult problem.*** You'll be asked this question to see how you interacted with a real-world situation, and what you perceive as being "difficult" — so don't be afraid to get real. Pull an actual example from the from your time at university or even your part-time job. Follow the brag story format to answer the question.

Let's move to a special call out, specifically if you're applying for consulting or business roles, similar to the Research Associate job description we reviewed in STEP 4.

For consulting jobs, you'll be asked a case study question. This could be an arbitrary question like,

STEP 6

"how many doors are there in Manhattan?" or *"how many fish are there in the sea?"*

Don't panic — there are no right or wrong answers for these types of questions. The goal is to understand how you would approach a broad and open-ended question and for you to showcase the interviewer your logic.

My recommendation with this arbitrary question is to ask follow/ clarifying questions first:

- *What do you mean by a door? Are we talking about interior doors or exterior doors? Is a door something that has a handle, which would mean elevator doors don't count?*

- Next verbalize assumptions or facts you would need to answer this question. For example,

    "if we assume Manhattan is 50 streets wide and 50 blocks long, and there are 10 buildings on each block. And each building averages 100 doors based on our agreed upon definition, then there'd be 50x50x100 doors in Manhattan, which equals 250,000…"

Another type of case study question could be a real-life project they're working on. For example, the interviewer may say *"we have a client that's interested in entering the single cell technology market. What information would you need to be able to inform the client whether this is a good or bad business opportunity?"* Again, there are no right or wrong answers here — the company wants to understand how you think and approach a question like this.

As before, also be sure to have your own questions ready and know who you should aim them at. For the HR person, you may ask about the company's culture, what they enjoy most about working at the company, or what type of candidate does well in this role/company.

For the hiring manager *(AKA your future boss)* — ask them what they expect the person who fills this role to complete in their first 100 days on the job, what onboarding is like, or who you'd be interacting with on a day-to-day basis.

If it's a peer you're interviewing with, ask them about your prospective manager's management style or what a typical day is like.

The day before your interview, I recommend you drive to the site so you can familiarize yourself with the route. And, ***on the day of your interview, give yourself plenty of time to get there!***

Try to get to the interview site about 20 minutes early. Turning up late makes for a terrible first impression — how will they trust you to be on time for work if you can't even be punctual to the interview?

STEP 6

If the interview is virtual — log in ahead of time, make sure your background is good (proper lighting, clean room, etc.), and be sure your camera and microphone work well.

Decide what you'll wear to the interview. Regardless of what the company dress code is, I always wear a suit because a suit makes me look professional — but you should use your best judgement.

I always get asked *what should I plan on bringing to the interview?* A safe approach is to plan on bringing a few copies of your resume, a pen and paper, and some printed copies of your previous work *(such as your senior thesis)* or a portfolio *(if applicable)*. But also have these things available if you are doing a virtual interview. You can always screen share to showcase your portfolio or senior thesis during the interview. Alternatively, you can always email them after the interview as part of your thank you note.

During the Job Interview

While the length of the interview will depend on how many people you're speaking with, assume you'll be there for at least 30 minutes per person. When your interviewer greets you, give them a firm handshake and repeat their name immediately after the introduction. Always say something along the lines of "it's great to meet you" — regardless of whether its in-person or online.

Try to get a business card from them as well *(you'll need their contact details to write thank you notes)*.

After running through your personal pitch, you'll be asked several questions — similar to the ones I listed above.

If you're unsure of an answer to a question, it's okay to say that you're unsure. They'd rather have you be honest than go off track with inaccurate answers. ***The most important thing to remember during the interview is to be yourself.*** Be as honest as you can — they'll respect you for that.

Always end by saying, *"Thank you for taking the time to talk with me. I'm confident that I'm a good fit for this role and I look forward to speaking with you soon."*

After the in-person job interview, **write a thank you note to everyone that you met**. If you didn't get any business cards — no problem. You should still send a thank you note to the recruiter with a request to pass it along to the team that interviewed you. Your thank you note doesn't need to be long. It should include:

- Saying thank you for their time,
- that you appreciated meeting them,
- something specific about the interview or items discussed. (For example, did you bond over a book or did you want to further explain your remarks to a question that was asked.),

STEP 6

- why you are excited about this opportunity/company, and
- a brief explanation of why you'd be a good fit for the job.

Remember to keep your thank you note short and to the point — it'll ensure you leave a great impression!

You may be called back for a second interview. And that's great — follow the same steps as above. If you're meeting an interviewer for the second time, think of new questions to ask and greet them accordingly.

So, to recap: A phone interview is often the start of the interview process and is generally with someone from the company's recruiting team. The in-person/virtual interviews are more comprehensive. The key to nailing both is to always be prepared —practice interview questions, both technical and soft-skill/behavioral questions. You've got this!

STEP 7:
Compensation and Negotiating the Offer

Many people forget that — when they're reviewing an offer — there's a lot more to consider than just the base salary.

What you should do is **pay attention to the whole compensation package**, which includes your base salary but also your annual bonus percentage, tuition reimbursement benefits, medical and dental benefits, paid-time-off, etc.

Some companies even offer things like discounted sport tickets or car insurance policies — so keep your eye out for these perks!

I always encourage folks to not get too hung up on the dollar value, but to have a deep look at everything the company is offering.

If a company is ready to make you an offer, they'll most likely call you and provide you the offer's details over the phone.

You have no obligation to accept anything on the spot, but you should respond with something along the lines of:

> *"Thank you so much for this opportunity — I'm really excited about the role. If it's okay with you, I'd like to review the whole compensation package. Can you send me an email with the offer letter and details about other benefits I'll receive like vacation time, tuition reimbursement, and medical?"*

Asking for the above in writing is common — it gives you a chance to review all the compensation details so you can make an informed decision rather than a judgment call on the spot.

Also, if you have multiple offers, you can compare and contrast them all against each other.

For the Associate Scientist I job description we reviewed in STEP 4, let's say that the company offers a Charlie Chemistry annual base salary of $55K. His first task is to figure out if that base salary is aligned with the industry average.

Some great sites to search for finding salary benchmarking information are: Glassdoor.com *(which can provide you company specific salary ranges),* Indeed.com, Salary.com, and Payscale.com. When

STEP 7

searching for salary benchmarks, try to be as specific as possible.

Make sure you look up information for the specific job title and a few related job titles *(job titles could vary from company to company, but the essential roles and responsibilities should be the same)*, the specific industry *(or even the specific company, if possible)*, size of the company, and region *(closest major city, no need to search for the exact location)*.

Many of these sites are free, but you may need to set up an account to access relevant information. One of the best things about these sites is that they provide more than just 1 salary number — they use a bell curve that shows a low- and high-end range and a median salary number.

For the Associate Scientist I role in Boston, MA, here are some *potential* search criteria Charlie could use to get the relevant salary benchmarks.

Search criteria:

- **Title:** Associate Scientist I, Entry Level Scientist, Entry level Chemist, etc.
- **Company Size:** >5001 employees
- **Years of Experience:** 0-2
- **Direct reports:** 0
- **Industry:** Biotech/Pharma

○ **Region:** Boston, MA area

Once Charlie has the salary data, I suggest he plots it to get a perspective of the range and the median. For the Associate Scientist I role in Boston, MA, data plotted from 4 different salary benchmark sites *could* look something like this:

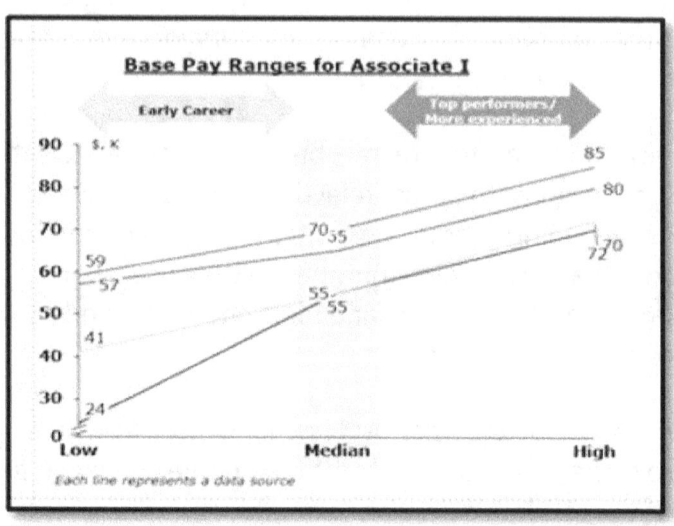

Each line represents a single data source. In this instance, a wide salary range exists for the Associate Scientist I role: $24k-85K. But it looks like the industry Median for this role is $55-70K.

Based on this information, Charlie can confirm that the company is offering a fair market base salary at $55K.

If, by chance, the company's offer came in lower than industry average (like $50K), I'd recommend Charlie

STEP 7

set up a time to speak over the phone with the HR person who made him the offer.

Never have a salary negation conversation over email. Since you're building a new relationship with the company, you don't want your tone to be misinterpreted through writing.

Once you're on the phone with the HR representative, be polite and to the point. Here's a recommended script you can use:

"Hi [NAME], thank you for sending me all this information. I can't describe how thankful I am to be given this opportunity and how excited I am about the role. However, I'm a little bit surprised by the offer — it's lower than I expected. Can you help me understand how you came up with this base salary figure?"

Now pause!

Pauses are important because it allows the other person to react to what you've just said. They're also an indication that you're calm, confident, and that you know your worth and how to negotiate.

In short — let the HR representative reply. Perhaps they'll tell you they used industry or internal benchmarks to arrive at the figure.

Once they've finished speaking, now is the time share that you've done your own research and your data suggests something different:

> *"Thank you for your explanation! Well, my research shows that the average salary range for this role is $55K to $70K. I'm more than happy to share my sources with you. All I'm asking is that I be paid fair market value.*

Again, pause.

Most likely, the HR partner will go back to the hiring manager to discuss your request.

If they don't budge, you may want to consider negotiating other aspects of your compensation package. Here's a tip — **everything is up for negotiation:** annual bonus percentage, timing of next salary review, your start date, when you'd be eligible for tuition reimbursement, etc.

Again, be polite through this process.

At the end of the day, the most important aspect of your first job is to get your foot in the door and gain necessary industry experience. But make sure you accept a salary that's realistic — you must be able to survive on it!

Let's consider another scenario, one in which you have 2 offers.

Company A is offering you more money, but you like the role and culture better at Company B. The good news is that you can use Company A's offer as leverage to negotiate your offer with Company B.

STEP 7

Set up a time to talk to Company B's HR representative to have an honest — but polite — conversation. Share that you are you have a higher offer from another company, but let them know that you would love to join Company B.

Then, ask if they can match Company A's offer. As long as Company A and Company B are in similar industries and the offer is for similar roles, in most cases, Company B will be happy to match the offer.

Know that it takes companies a significant amount of time and money to find the right candidate. They will unlikely want to lose talent because of a $5K base salary difference.

Once you have verbally accepted the job offer, you'll want to outline your start date.

Try to pick a date 2 weeks from the day you officially accepted the offer. The 2-week notice is the average length of time to notify a part-time employer that you're going to take on a new role.

This is a courtesy as you'll give your manager ample time to fill your position or come up with a plan on how to disperse the work across other employees.

During the two weeks, still show up on time, continue to have a strong work-ethic to wrap any on-going projects, and provide necessary support to ensure a smooth transition.

You never know when you'll have to ask your part-time manager to be a reference again, so best to leave with your best foot forward.

So, to recap: Compensation is more than just your annual base salary number. Make sure you do your research on salary benchmarks. Be confident and polite in your negotiations. Know your worth and don't settle for a company who won't pay you what you deserve! Give your part-time employer at least a 2 week notice before transitioning to your new job.

STEP 8:
References, Background, and Drug Checks

Ah, the last step in the process! Congrats on making it to final part of your journey.

Now that you've verbally accepted your offer, it's likely that your acceptance is contingent on a reference, background, and *(sometimes)* a drug test.

Let's start with the ***drug test*** since this is a crucial step in the hiring process for any position and one where you'll need to be proactive, *well before you even get a job offer.*

Pre-employment drug screening helps companies mitigate risks, since hiring an applicant who uses drugs could jeopardize the company's reputation and can also be costly *(due to absenteeism, workman compensation claims, or even legal ramifications)*. The drug test is typically a urine, saliva, blood, or hair test done at an off-site, preapproved health clinic.

A good rule of thumb is to stay clean throughout your whole job search!

Most recreational drugs can stay in your system for months and can be detected on a drug test — even if you stopped while you were interviewing.

Don't let a failed drug test be what keeps you from starting your dream STEM job.

Now that's out the way, let's move on.

Some companies may do a formal ***background check*** on you. This includes a Criminal Offender Record Information (CORI) check which lists any criminal cases you've been involved in within the state. A background check may also include a credit check to see if you have any major outstanding debts. *(I'm talking about tens of thousands of dollars — or more — of credit card debt.)*

The good news is that your college loans don't count.

I'm sure the background check is nothing to worry about. However, if you're concerned, be honest and upfront with your future employer — no matter how painful it may be. For example, if you were caught shoplifting when you were 18, let your employer know that this may show up on your background check, even if all charges were dropped. It's best to disclose and explain the situation rather than hiding it. *(It's way worse if they find out from a source that isn't you!)*

Lastly, a background check will often include verifying everything on your resume. Employers will sometimes hire third party companies to validate every claim on your resume — where you worked, how long you worked there, what your title was, and whether you really did attend XYZ University and graduate with a degree in ABC.

In short, **tell the truth on your resume**.

Also, if your college or previous employer had a name change, make sure you note it on your resume to avoid confusion. For example, I have an MBA from Simmons College. However, Simmons College became Simmons University in 2018. I've made a note of the name change on my resume.

References: Most employers will ask for at least 2 references from people who you've worked with in the past, preferably in a professional capacity *(so your mom, best friend, and next-door neighbor don't count)*. This is where your college professors and your manager at your part-time job will come in handy.

Remember, your references are doing you a favor so make it easy for them to speak on your behalf.

Start by sending them an email to let them know you've been offered a role at XYZ company, attach your resume and the job description to the email, and ask them if they'd be comfortable being a reference for you.

If they say yes, then confirm what the best contact information for the company is to reach you *(preferably a phone number and email address)*.

So, to recap: Stay clean throughout your job search *(start now!),* tell the truth on your resume because it will come up on your background check, and make it easy for your previous employers/college professors to be a reference for you.

Final Word

Well, my friend, we have come to the end of our journey. Thank you for letting me be your guide!

Congrats on landing your new job. After your first day *(and after you've signed all the paperwork that makes you an official employee),* update your LinkedIn profile with the title and company details of your new role. You may also want to change your summary since you now have a job.

If you found this book useful *(or even if you didn't)* please leave me a review on Amazon.

I'm always looking for ways to improve the process, make it easier for the next round of graduates, and to let them know that there is help out there.

Lastly, check out my website: www.thecareerlabformula.com for additional resources, like:

- ***"Brag stories" template*** to help you to contextualize your work experience stories into the "challenge, action, result" framework

- ***Career profiles:*** read about people's STEM career journey, their biggest career mistakes, and what advice they have for recent graduates

- ***Mastering your onboarding:*** beyond just the tools you need to do your job, but the people whom you need to meet

- ***The 100-day reflection worksheet:*** how to get valuable, guided feedback from your new manager

- And much more!

APPENDIX:
Sample Areas of Employment By Degree Type

Degree	Sample Employment Areas
Aerospace Engineering	- Aircraft certification and accident investigation authorities
- Aerospace design and manufacturing industry
- Airline and space operations
- Government research laboratories

Biology/ Biological Engineering	· Business Development · Consulting firms · Environmental Organizations · Food and Beverage Manufacturers · Government/ Health Departments · Health Care · Laboratories · Law and Drug Enforcement · Law Firms · Pharma/biotech, Medical device, and Life Science Companies · Product Management · Publishing companies · Research Institutes · Sales
Biomedical Engineering	· Development of health care technologies · Educational institutions · Engineering Consulting · Investment Banking · Healthcare establishments · Management Consulting · Medical Device Companies · Medical facilities · Venture capital firms

APPENDIX

Chemistry/ Chemical Engineering	· Lab technology · Manufacturing · Marketing · Product Development · Project Management · Research and Development · Risk Management · Sales · Quality Assurance
Civil Engineering	· Construction Firms · Engineering Design/Consulting Firms · Geotechnical/Foundation Engineering · Municipalities and Other Levels of Government · Project Management · Research and Development · Sanitary Services · Transportation Industry · Urban and Municipal Planning · Water Resources

Computer Science	- Analytics & Data Scientist - Communications - Consulting - Database Administration - Digital Marketing - Digital Strategy - E-commerce - Financial Quality Assurance - Identity and Access Management - Information Technology - Investment Banking - Mobile app development - Network Security/ Cyber Security - Network Testing - Project Management - Software and Computing Services - Software development/ engineering - Tech based Venture Capital - Technology Development
Electrical Engineering	- Consumer Electronics - Control and Instrumentation Systems - Digital Signal Processing - Electrical Energy Production and Transmission - Fiber Optics and Laser Design - Integrated Circuits - Internet and Computer Technologies - Telecommunication

APPENDIX

Health Sciences	- Community and Social Services - Consulting - Genetics - Global/International Health - Health and Safety - Health Program Evaluation - Health Promotion Coordinator - Health Research - Healthcare and Regulatory Systems - Human Resources - Healthcare Services - Law - Media and Communication
Math/ Statistics	- Actuarial Sciences - Analytics and Data Services - Business Development - Business or Financial Analysis - Consulting - Cryptographer - Database Administration - eCommerce - Financial Services - Fund Manager - Market Research - Project Management - Pricing Analyst - Policy Analysis - Program Analysis - Risk Management - Underwriting

Mechanical Engineering	<ul><li>Administration</li><li>Building services and plant engineering</li><li>Consulting engineering firms</li><li>Educational institutions</li><li>Energy utilities</li><li>Government and industry laboratories</li><li>Manufacturing industry</li><li>Transportation industry</li></ul>
Nanoscience	<ul><li>Auto and aerospace industries</li><li>Biotechnology</li><li>Electronics</li><li>Energy capture and storage</li><li>Environmental monitoring, control, and remediation</li><li>Food science</li><li>Forensics</li><li>Industrial Manufacturers</li><li>Materials science including textiles, polymers, packaging, among others</li><li>Medical Equipment/Devices</li><li>Medical fields and pharmaceuticals</li><li>Military and national security</li><li>Nuclear/Energy</li><li>Pharmaceutical</li><li>Quality Control and Inspection Companies</li><li>Research & Development</li><li>Sporting goods companies</li></ul>

APPENDIX

Physics	<ul><li>Applied Research and Development</li><li>Consulting</li><li>Government Research and Regulation</li><li>Healthcare Sector – Medical Device Development</li><li>Hi-tech Industry</li></ul>

About the Author

Siddhi Shah has over 15 years of achievement in Corporate Strategy and Strategic Marketing within the Life Sciences, Pharma/Biotech, and Consulting industries. Knowing she only could have achieved this with the help of amazing mentors, Siddhi now enjoys coaching the next generation of recent STEM graduates as they transition into the workforce. Siddhi also previously volunteered her time as a mentor on CareerContessa.com and as a Board Member at Project Learn. She holds a BS from MIT, an MEng from UPenn, and an MBA from Simmons School of Management. Siddhi currently lives in the greater Boston area with her husband and son.

www.ingramcontent.com/pod-product-compliance
Lightning Source LLC
Chambersburg PA
CBHW071129240526
45465CB00024B/1552